SILENT ECHOES

Poetry

Ahaana Goswamy

Published By

Anybook

Cell : 9971698930

E-mail : contactanybook@gmail.com

Website : www.anybook.org

First published by Anybook in 2023

Copyright © 2023 Ahaana Goswamy

Printed and bound in India

Cover Design & Typesetting by Anybook

ISBN : 978-93-91571-97-9

Dedication

"To the meaningless thoughts that added up to form beautiful phrases"

PREFACE

As I stand on the precipice of the unknown, my words become my refuge. In this collection,

you'll find the essence of my being—a senior's journey from despair to creative illumination.

Poems

Poems

1.

She hides herself behind her pretty smile

Assuring people that she is completely fine

But those who know the real her

Know that she cries herself to sleep Every night!!

She is a work of art

haunted by her inner demons

They paint her life on a canvas

Red paint splashes on the black screen

As they whisper In her ear

Tormenting her day and night

Weak she gets with every passing breath

Holding onto the hope that she can't paint

With each passing second

The layers add up

Pink, Blue, Purple skies fade Away

Orange sunsets appear grey

Her canvas ruins her life by mixing in the wrong colors

She is now tired of painting her sky black

No more silver drops, no more violet screams

She weaves a beautiful web

but paints it her darkest green
Sadistic thoughts cloud her mind
As she holds the brush in her hand
strokes her head, a shade of red
But deep down she cries for help

2.

Save me for my brain's too-cruel
Seems as if my enemy's been implanted in me
Never agreeing, always provoking
All rash decisions are its judgement
Mind's been convinced too, but some goodness is still left
For sometimes it takes my side
Brain conquers the spirit and the soul
Tortures me from within
And then fakes a smile
So that no one else would know
How clever, how witty
Whom do I go and cry to
About the internal battles
When you graze my skull with the tip of your sword
Sharpened after every blow
You carve your wonders at night
When the darkness is too much
I gulp
I know the moon has given you its power
I know you've been recharged

I beg you; let me live
Be a little merciful
But you see the drapes of the curtains around my bed
Force me to think of the pain
Strangle me by wrapping them around my neck
Tests for how long I can hold my breath,
By drowning me in the bathroom sink
All I can see is blue
All I can do is gasp
The salt streams have dried now
The redness is too evident
Before I completely finish myself
You allow me to unwrap it
You move your forceful arm from my head so I can
look up and breathe
It's torture and you being the master of all sadists,
do it repeatedly
My stars bear all the faults of this world, don't
they?
That's why you punish me whenever I get angry
How dare I
After all, I am the one who's responsible
For the calamities taking place outside

3.

I am internally begging
Begging your soul for attention
But your conscience is oblivious to my plea
Turning your head the other way, you laugh
Knowing the power you have over me
One cry and I'll be on my knees
Attending to your every need
Then you'll say you love me three thousand
Making my innocent heart weep,
Not because I am weak or because I am vulnerable
But because I know I'll have to fight
Why is it so hard to maintain your love?
Does everyone need to work this way?
Or are you just asking for too much?
Is it normal for you to take away all that you give?
Especially when I least expect it
Or do you just call this a sport?
A sport that you invented to play with people's minds
and fuck up their souls
But you'll apologize at the end of it, won't you?

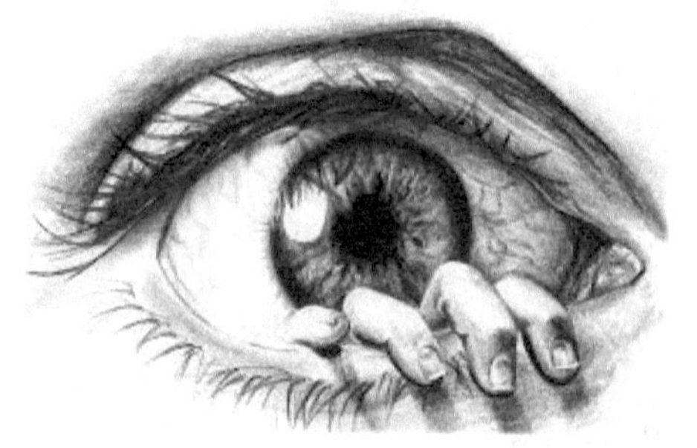

You'll weave those beautiful words and make a spider's
net
trapping me once again
And I'll be on my knees
Serving your soul
Like it's a treasure made of gold

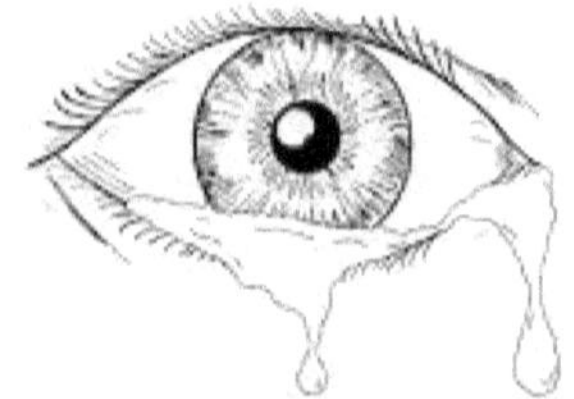

4.

Can't you see I am silently screaming for help?
Have I not made it so indirectly obvious?
Oh, wait...Communication is key, right?
I think I need to spell it out for you, then:
I am NOT OKAY!
I need you!
I am not sure where the connection broke
Maybe it didn't break completely; it just went off
It'll come back, I am sure
It'll come back tomorrow, I know it
It didn't?
How could that happen?
Has it not always returned?
Has it stopped calling my demons its home?
What is happening?
It's all going haywire!
I thought we were friends!
Now you don't even get why I call you thrice a day just to utter 30 seconds later
"Imma call you back"
Haven't you noticed

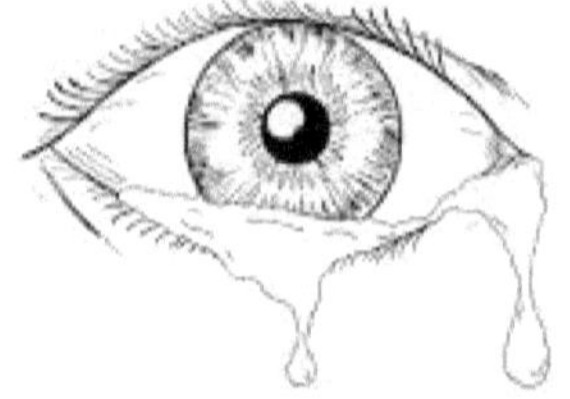

I stopped saying "I love you" before cutting your call
Oh wait...I know!
You noticed;
But you accepted I had changed and you moved on...
Classic!
But why don't we address my stupid insecurities
anymore?
I need you to scream at me for "not having any faith in
you"
I need you to whisper 'Afterglow' in my ear
With my head on your lap
Your hand on my head
Patting me down
Into a deep slumber
I'll be okay not waking up ever again
Just give me closure
One last time
Talk to me if something feels off
I'll listen to you holding me accountable for the changed
behaviors
I'll accept it and I'll move on
After all
Communication is key,
right?

———————

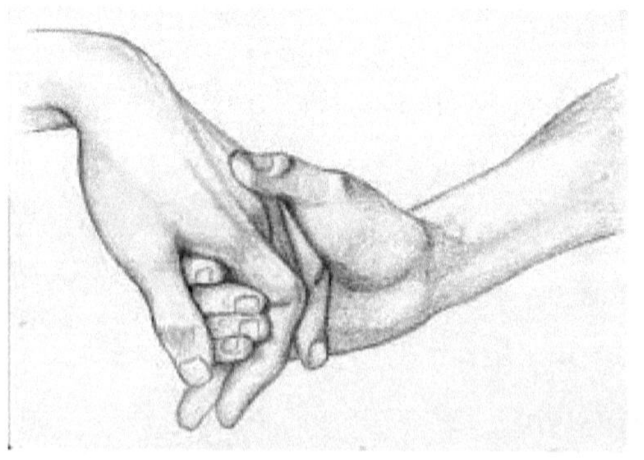

5.

I don't know if we are meant for this
But Baby we could be it
We can be endgame if we stop playing our own games
Stop pretending, start reinventing
New things to say each day
Make you more loved than you thought ever possible
Give it a thought
Do you really see us as impossible
Come on, don't lie
Cause I know what lies in your heart
I know it's not red
But it also ain't dark
So come and take my hand
We'll figure out things as we go
For now, it's enough to know
That we'll be there for each other
Through the highs and the lows

6.

You said you'll remember
Dunno who you were
And it's all just a blur
The world spins around me
I feel dizzy
Calling softly
Feel the ground shift beneath me
And I'm falling headlong into the deep dark sea
Your wave overwhelms me
Drowning me deep underneath,
I can't resurface
Oh, please! Let me breathe

7.

One hug can do wonders
I realized in that moment
One hug was all I was craving
In that desolate state
Blurry vision, hyperventilation
Constant tears; blood-red eyes
Couldn't breathe
A thousand thoughts just running through my mind
Flashing, vanishing then reappearing
It seemed they had a pattern
Teasing, torturing, scare-ing, scarring me
Afraid, no one there; alone in my room I laid
Just thinking of that one person
Their hug that I craved
The one that warmed my heart; calmed me and kept all
negative thoughts at bay
The one whose vibe matched mine like no one else's

I could fall asleep in that warm embrace!!!

8.

An awkward silence
The beginning of every conversation
It's not always a pick-up line
It's not always a crazy sign
Sometimes when you are meant to be
You find the path that leads into the spotlight
where you two meet

9.

She doesn't care
It is all in there
Her weaknesses; her promises
She gets scared
She disappears
Believing no one cares for her
Her eyes are red, puffed and shut
Eccentricity is in her blood
Her thoughts are clouded, burdening her
Her mind, she feels
Crumbling inside
Consumed by her own self

10.

I told him a thousand secrets, he told me a thousand lies
His voice was my lullaby
But now it sounds like a criminal's cry
How could he so easily put all this blame on me
and think that I feel relief
When all I felt was pain
It broke my heart again and again
And now I stand here on this street
Gazing at the stars
Wondering if you ever knew who I was
Or was I just supposed to be your shadow
Following your lead, in the dark

11.

All this time spent together
Did we ever know each other
All mind games, you mansplained
Should we have communicated?
You made me crazy, now something has come over me
Zipped my tongue, cause I could hear it in my head
I thought I was your someone blue
But now I am your someone old
and you have your someone new

To carry your thoughts home

12.

Every time I see the way you look at me

I die, die of the thought

What if I lose the look I see?

It'll break my heart

Damaged; broken goods

Aren't we all the same at the end

Don't compare the beginnings

People follow twisted roads

Some overlap for life, some for a short span of time

In the end, all that matters is

whether you made it out of the maze

Whether you touched the victory cup first

Because people don't compare paths

They don't see who got it easier

They just care about the end

Exhaust yourself; Starve yourself; torture yourself

But don't give up

Work till it hurts to even speak

But Don't Give Up!!!

13.

I think I am happier being the moon
Being appreciated for my beauty instead of
being hated for my heat
The depth of my unexplored craters prove

more fatal than the merciless wrath of the sun

14.

I know how to lay still
Mirroring the silence of the night
When the moon shines its brightest blue
and the stars' flicker overpowers the darkness of the sky

15.

I speak too loud

But I cry ever so softly

Do you think I am afraid of being seen as weak?

No!

I just can't let my tears declare defeat

16.

I have been an ocean all my life
Full of depth, darkness and beauty
Mystical creatures reside on the surface
Watch them from afar but dive into the waters
Only if you have the will to meet the demonic species
that lie deep within
Swim to the bottom and say hello
Deeds done!

Now you can call me your home

17.

In the wrecked boat lay the ruins of my once-home

Now the water slowly seeps in

Engulfing the wooden structure

As it peacefully drowns into the darkness of the still blue waters

That once supported the sole weight of my soul

18.

She kills with mere words
That's her strongest weapon
So sweet yet so sharp
And most importantly
UNFORESEEN

19.

Fragments glued together
To create beautiful archways
That now weave the path
To your very own

Red Carpet!!!

20.

You seem so bright and beautiful to the world outside
Shining ever so strongly
But only those who have proved capable enough to reach
you
Are aware of the craters that lie
Deep within your surface

21.

Hurricanes bring thunderstorms and dark clouds

But those who have endured the weather for long enough

Walk smoothly in the presence of their new home

22.

There's no room for the weak in this world

Maybe that's the reason why

All havens reside behind closed doors

23.

Humans have the tendency to love the things
that cause them the most pain
How else will words ever create art?
If you loved someone who didn't make your tears
scream your dreams
like silent echoes of the night
How would there ever be poetry again?

If you fell in love with the person and not the idea

24.

The soul weeps as the world benefits

Envisioning the broken pieces

That people call "the beauty within"

25.

You can't weave beauty with your words
If you aren't dealing with thunderstorms in your brain
How will I ever paint your portrait in my heart

if I haven't seen your truest shades of grey

26.

What if heaven and hell
coexist on this very planet
Instead of being two realms
on the opposite ends?
Every deed you do weaves your route
towards Satan or
Crumples to kindle the light that guides you towards
the angels

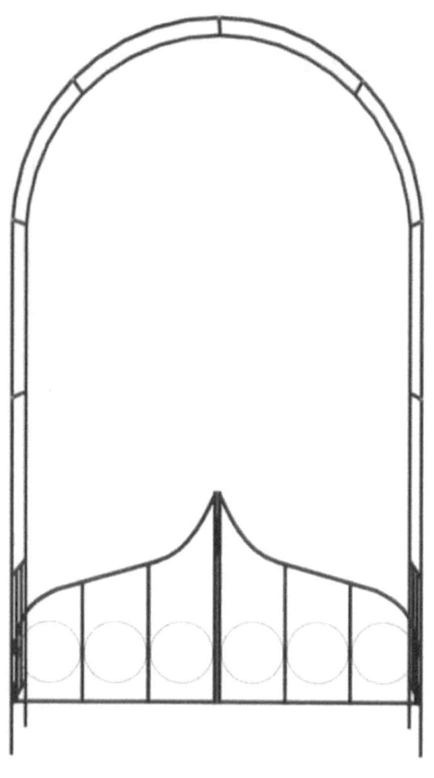

27.

As you inhale the air of the ghost town

Do you gain a part of them?

Merge it with your soul?

Pronounce it like a treasure?

Announce it to the world?

Do you visit this ghost town often?....

.....Just to get a whiff of their shadow?

Do you ever wish to undo turning their love into a

wasteland

Just to get a glimpse of the broken memories??

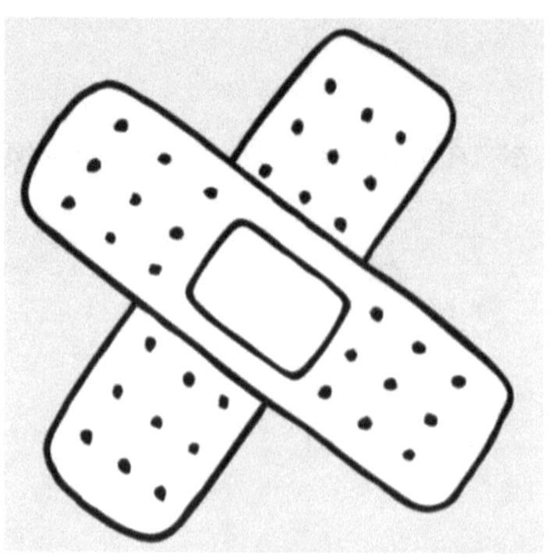

28.

In a world where trauma never ceases to exist, is it fair
to call its terms acceptable?
Negotiate all you want, but can you ever justify its
conditions?
Yes you deserved better, that's all they said, didn't they?
But they were your true friends, so they knew what
they were talking about!
I guess they did, otherwise why would you call a person
your home instead of your childhood house
The walls were painted white just so they could hide the
darkest shades of grey
The elders did a splendid job of hiding the wounds of
their childhood
Just to reveal the band-aids later
Which WE ripped off????
How ironic!!
Some battles are better left unhandled, because the

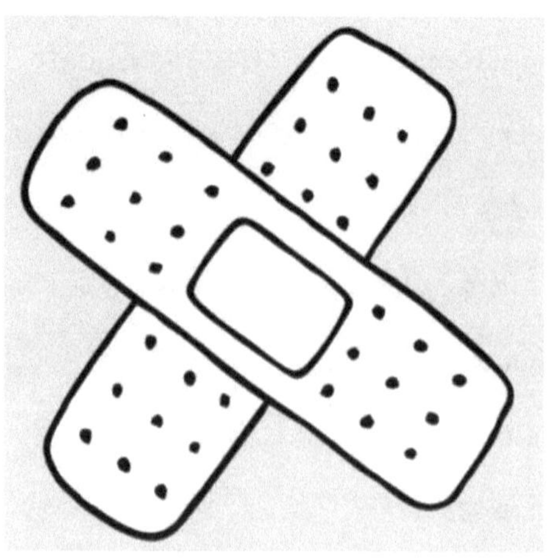

adults always have trauma as their secret weapon

Hiding in the darkest alleys of the basements which they

(by the way) do call home

And I wonder why they never ask for rent, for sharing

their home with us

I guess that's the price we pay for living off of their

money for 18 years, don't we?

Therapy sessions; years later; we pay paycheck after

paycheck to heal our wounds properly

Because that's all we ever learned

To never slap a band-aid on cuts that had the potential

to bleed endlessly